SNOWMOBILING

APEX

BY HUBERT WALKER

WWW.APEXEDITIONS.COM

Apex is distributed by North Star Editions:
sales@northstareditions.com | 888-417-0195

Produced for Apex by Red Line Editorial.

Photographs ©: Liz Copan/The Gazette/AP Images, cover (snowmobile), 1 (snowmobile); Pixabay, cover (background), 1 (background); Shutterstock Images, 4–5, 6–7, 8–9, 10–11, 12, 13, 14–15, 16–17, 20, 21, 22–23, 24–25, 26, 27, 29; iStockphoto, 18, 19

Library of Congress Control Number: 2021915740

ISBN
978-1-63738-156-4 (hardcover)
978-1-63738-192-2 (paperback)
978-1-63738-262-2 (ebook pdf)
978-1-63738-228-8 (hosted ebook)

Printed in the United States of America
Mankato, MN
012022

NOTE TO PARENTS AND EDUCATORS

Apex books are designed to build literacy skills in striving readers. Exciting, high-interest content attracts and holds readers' attention. The text is carefully leveled to allow students to achieve success quickly. Additional features, such as bolded glossary words for difficult terms, help build comprehension.

TABLE OF CONTENTS

CHAPTER 1

SNOCROSS

Snowmobile riders wait at the starting line. Soon, the green light flashes. The riders take off in a flurry of snow.

Snowmobile races can have 10 or more riders.

The snowmobile engines buzz loudly. The riders go over jump after jump. Snow sprays behind them as they turn around corners.

Snocross racers have to land jumps without getting hurt.

Snocross is based on motocross. But racers use snowmobiles instead of motorcycles.

Snocross races often involve many laps around a track.

Two riders crash, but the others speed past them. Soon, the riders are on their final lap. The winner pumps his fist as he crosses the finish line.

SNOCROSS TRACKS

Snocross tracks have many jumps and bumps. A whoop section is the part of the track with several small bumps in a row. The finish line is usually a big jump.

CHAPTER 2

SNOWMOBILE HISTORY

People built the first snowmobiles in the early 1900s. Back then, snowmobiles were just sleds with skis on them. Some riders used ropes for steering.

One early snowmobile came out in the 1910s. It was a car that had skis added to it.

The first **modern** snowmobiles came out in the 1950s. **Professional** racing began a few years later. Some races took place in farm fields. Others were at fairgrounds.

The 1960 Ski-Doo was going to be called "Ski-Dog." But there was a typing mistake.

Snowmobile riders race in Eagle River, Wisconsin.

Some early snowmobiles used airplane propellers for power.

EAGLE RIVER

Eagle River, Wisconsin, is known as the home of snowmobiling. The first race took place there in 1964. The town still hosts the World **Championship** every year.

Snowmobiling continued to spread. And snowmobiles kept getting more powerful.

By the late 1980s, some snowmobiles could go 160 miles per hour (257 km/h).

Snowmobiles today can have engines as powerful as the ones in cars.

CHAPTER 3

SNOWMOBILE RACING

There are several kinds of snowmobile racing. Snocross is one of the most popular. Riders go around sharp turns. They also go over jumps.

Snocross pros are able to turn corners without losing speed.

Drag racing is popular, too. In these races, riders go in a straight line. Riders can reach speeds of more than 190 miles per hour (306 km/h).

Snowmobile drag races last just seconds.

Drag-racing tracks tend to be 660 feet (201 m) long.

Drag racing usually takes place on ice instead of snow.

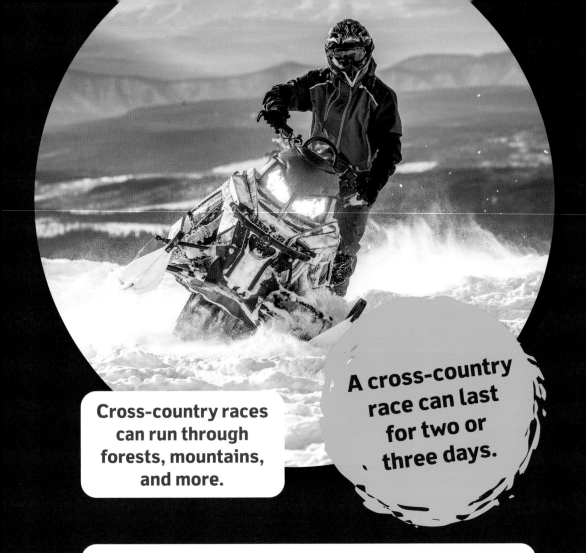

Cross-country races can run through forests, mountains, and more.

A cross-country race can last for two or three days.

Cross-country is the most grueling type of snowmobile racing. Riders race for hundreds of miles. These races often involve teams of riders.

RACING CATEGORIES

Snowmobile races are split into different **categories**. The fastest snowmobiles are grouped together. Also, adults and kids race separately. That way, races are fairer.

A parent and child get ready to compete in their own snowmobile races.

CHAPTER 4

SNOWMOBILE FREESTYLE

Not all snowmobile riders take part in races. Some **compete** in snowmobile freestyle events. In these events, style is more important than speed.

Snowmobile freestyle started becoming popular in the 2000s.

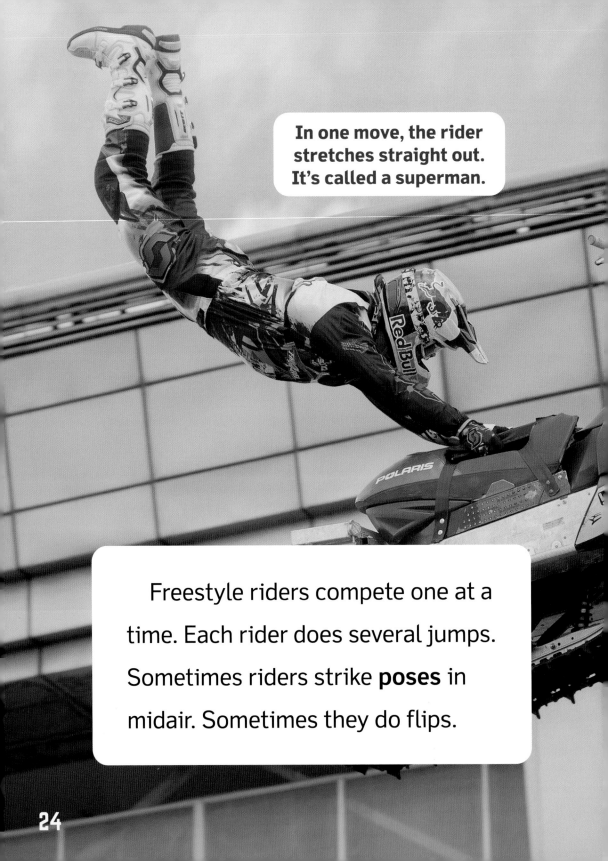

In one move, the rider stretches straight out. It's called a superman.

Freestyle riders compete one at a time. Each rider does several jumps. Sometimes riders strike **poses** in midair. Sometimes they do flips.

Each freestyle rider gets 75 seconds to do tricks.

Judges watch the riders. They give riders points. Difficult tricks are worth more points. The rider with the most points is the winner.

Helmets keep snowmobilers' heads safe. They also keep heads warm in cold weather.

Flips are some of the toughest freestyle tricks. They can also be very dangerous.

SAFETY GEAR

Snowmobile riders must stay safe. They wear helmets on their heads. They also wear kneepads and chest pads. When crashes happen, safety gear **reduces** the risk of injury.

COMPREHENSION QUESTIONS

Write your answers on a separate piece of paper.

1. Write a few sentences explaining the main ideas of Chapter 3.

2. Which type of snowmobile race would you want to compete in? Why?

3. Which type of snowmobile rider goes in a straight line?

> **A.** snocross
> **B.** drag racing
> **C.** cross-country

4. Why do kids and adults take part in different races?

> **A.** so adults do not have to teach kids how to ride
> **B.** so kids have a fair chance of winning races
> **C.** so the racetracks are not too crowded

5. What does **hosts** mean in this book?

*The first race took place there in 1964. The town still **hosts** the World Championship every year.*

    A. sets up an event

    B. wins a race

    C. goes to a new city

6. What does **grueling** mean in this book?

*Cross-country is the most **grueling** type of snowmobile racing. Riders race for hundreds of miles.*

    A. easy and fun

    B. difficult and tiring

    C. short and fast

Answer key on page 32.

GLOSSARY

categories
Groups of races for riders of certain ages, vehicles, or skill levels.

championship
A contest that decides a winner.

compete
To try to beat others in a game or event.

modern
Using new and improved ideas and tools.

motocross
A type of motorcycle racing that takes place on dirt tracks.

poses
Ways of holding the body, especially when doing a trick or having one's picture taken.

professional
Having to do with people who get paid for what they do.

propellers
Spinning blades that make vehicles go.

reduces
Makes something less likely.

TO LEARN MORE

BOOKS

Abdo, Kenny. *Snocross*. Minneapolis: Abdo Publishing, 2018.

Katirgis, Jane, and Bob Woods. *Racing Snowmobiles*. New York: Enslow Publishing, 2018.

Wiseman, Blaine. *Snowmobiling*. New York: AV2 by Weigl, 2021.

ONLINE RESOURCES

Visit **www.apexeditions.com** to find links and resources related to this title.

ABOUT THE AUTHOR

Hubert Walker enjoys running, hunting, and going to the dog park with his best pal. He grew up in Georgia but moved to Minnesota in 2018. Overall, he loves his new home, but he's not a fan of the cold winters.

INDEX

Answer Key:
1. Answers will vary; **2.** Answers will vary; **3.** B; **4.** B; **5.** A; **6.** B